D0975043

You Don't Know What War Is

The Diary of a Young Girl from Ukraine

YEVA SKALIETSKA

UNION
SQUARE
& CO.

NEW YORK

**UNION
SQUARE
&CO.**

NEW YORK

UNION SQUARE & CO. and the distinctive Union Square & Co. logo
are trademarks of Sterling Publishing Co., Inc.

Union Square & Co., LLC, is a subsidiary of Sterling Publishing Co., Inc.

This book is based upon the author's memories and recollections of events.
However, the names and identifying characteristics of certain individuals
have been changed to protect their privacy.

ISBN 978-1-4549-4969-5
ISBN 978-1-4549-4970-1 (e-book)

For information about custom editions, special sales, and premium purchases,
please contact specialsales@unionsquareandco.com.

Printed in Canada

2 4 6 8 10 9 7 5 3 1

unionsquareandco.com

Cover illustration and design: Kimberly Glyder
Interior design: Kevin Ullrich

Additional picture credits: Shutterstock.com/grebeshkovmaxim (map): vi;
© 2022 Anonymous, 37.

Contents

A map of Ukraine and its major cities, and the countries surrounding it, showing the journey Yeva and her grandmother Iryna took after fleeing Kharkiv.

Prologue

Everyone knows the word *war*. But very few people understand what it truly means. You might say that it's horrible and frightening, but you don't know the scale of fear it brings. And so, when you suddenly find you have to face it, you feel totally lost, walled in by fright and despair. All of your plans are suddenly interrupted by destruction. Until you've been there, you don't know what war is.

I am surrounded by flowers, gift bags, and a big balloon as I celebrate my twelfth birthday on February 14, 2022.

Before

My Birthday

I wake up early on the morning of February 14. Today is my birthday. I'm twelve! Almost a teenager! There's a surprise in my room: balloons! Five of them! There's a silver one, a pink one, a gold one, and even a couple of turquoise ones. I feel excited knowing there will be more surprises to come.

Messages are popping up on my phone from people wishing me a happy birthday. Seven people have already texted before I leave for school. I'm eager to get there.

When I get to class, everyone is stopping in the corridor to say "happy birthday" to me. I smile from ear to ear all day long. My face actually starts to hurt. I'm planning to celebrate my birthday on Saturday and am having a bowling party at Nikolsky Mall. I've given out the invitations and everyone is excited.

I arrive home from school. I live with my Granny Iryna, but when Mom comes to visit from Turkey, I stay with her at my other grandparents', Granny Zyna and Granddad Yosip. Mom's here for my birthday, but Dad lives and works abroad and couldn't come this time. Granny Iryna, my aunt and uncle, and my little cousin come over for a special birthday meal of snacks and sandwiches. I play a waltz by Tchaikovsky and Beethoven's "Für Elise" on the piano. Everyone listens; it feels very peaceful.

Then we have our snacks and sandwiches. The best was the tasty cake with candles on it!

The day has finally come. We are going bowling! I love bowling so much. Throwing balls. Getting high scores. Having fun! We arrive and I meet up with my friends. Many of them give me gifts of money. But one of my classmates really goes above and beyond. . . . He gives me a beautiful bouquet of flowers and a small, elegant, Italian-made silver chain with a pendant. The joy I feel has no bounds. I thank him a million times. I hope he sees the sincerity in my eyes.

We start the game. I'm first. I'm doing very well because I've been bowling before. I feel quite competitive. I enjoy throwing the ball, and I'm impatient for my turn to come around again. Olha is doing great too. Kostya launches the ball at the speed of light, but he doesn't seem to care about the direction he's throwing it in, so he's not having a good time. I win one or two rounds. Taras has a very curious approach. He thinks he'll get a strike if he makes a running start, and it actually ends up working. But in the end, despite my competitive spirit, it doesn't really matter who wins; it's just nice to be together.

Then comes the next day. On February 20, Mom goes back to Turkey. I've spent most of my life living with Granny Iryna. And we're very happy together, just the two of us.

My life is busy. I attend an English class twice a week, and I am really enjoying learning the language. Every Sunday, I go down to the city center for my piano lessons. I pass old houses with large windows, and the Wedding Palace, which was built in 1920. The thing I like most about it here is all the shops.

Kharkiv has loads of beautiful places. The city center, the Shevchenko City Garden, the zoo, and Gorky Park. The Shevchenko Garden is especially beautiful and has an amazing musical fountain with toy monkeys playing different instruments. There's also a really cool dolphinarium nearby where you can go visit dolphins and beluga whales. There is a beautifully paved street that leads up to Derzhprom, a group of tall buildings in Freedom Square. And whenever Granny and I need to soothe our souls, we visit the Svya-to-Pokrovs'kyy Monastery.

I am happy at school. I really enjoy learning and having a laugh with my friends.

I always try not to be late for my classes. I really love the breaks between classes, especially the longer ones, because I always have tons of fun with my best friends, Evhen and Olha. We run wild around the school, spinning around like little helicopters. My favorite subjects are geography, math, English, and German. Once school is over, my friends and I walk home together.

I love my room in Granny Iryna's apartment. It's very cozy, with really comfy armchairs. I do my homework on a cute little desk. I've got my easel and my oil paints right in

the middle of the room. Whenever I feel inspired, I sit down and paint. On my bed, I always have my favorite stuffed animal—a pink cat. It is long (like a sausage) and white-bellied, and I call it Chupapelya. I don't know why I named her that, or what it even means, but it just stuck.

The windows in my room look out toward the city, and the windows in Granny's bedroom face the Russian border and some houses and huge empty fields.

Granny's apartment has a big kitchen filled with Italian furniture. There's a tall palm tree in a pot in the corner. We have a lot of plants. Also, I really enjoy taking nice warm baths in our huge tub with massage jets. It's such a lovely apartment and in a great neighborhood in a block of buildings on the northeastern outskirts of Kharkiv.

I often have lots of homework. Once I'm done with it, I turn on the TV. And then I fall into a carefree sleep.

And that's how life is. Sure, there have been some rumors and murmurings about Russia, but they are just that: words. Life on February 14 is normal. And on the fifteenth, sixteenth, seventeenth . . . and up until the early hours of February 24, 2022. My life is peaceful.

꙰

OPPOSITE: Me in my room before the war, in front of my comfy armchairs (top), and painting at my easel (bottom).

UKRAINE

"'You Need to Get Up, the War Has Started'—
Voices from Kharkiv"

—*Washington Post*, February 24, 2022, 5:00 a.m.

Day 1

The Beginning

The night of February 24, 2022, had been very ordinary. I had slept soundly. But then, for some reason, I suddenly woke up at five in the morning. I decided to leave my bedroom and try sleeping in the living room. I lay on the couch, closed my eyes, and started drifting off.

5:10 a.m. I was woken suddenly by a loud metallic sound that echoed through the streets. At first, for some reason, I thought it was a car being crushed into scrap metal, which is weird because I don't live near a scrap metal site, but I didn't give it much thought.

Then I realized it was an explosion.

I saw Granny standing by the window, looking toward the Russian border. She was watching Grad missiles flying over the fields. All of a sudden, a massive rocket flew by and exploded with such force that I felt my heart go cold in my chest.

Car alarms were going off. Granny was trying to stay calm. She came over, saying, "Is Putin really starting a war with Ukraine?"

Yes. It seemed he was. I was in complete shock. I didn't know what to say. I knew Granny was telling the truth, but it was very hard to believe. I'd grown up hearing about war, but I'd never been in one. I was terrified.

We didn't have time to think. No one had told us what we should do if a war broke out. None of us were prepared for a war. Not me, not Granny, not our neighbors. We just knew we had to leave the apartment and get to the nearest basement.

My hands were shaking, my teeth rattling. I felt fear all around me. I realized I was having my first-ever panic attack. Granny kept trying to calm me down, telling me I needed to focus. She put a cross pendant around my neck and then put her jewelry box away in the wardrobe.

I checked my phone. A discussion about what was happening had broken out on our school chat.

Once we were ready, we ran out onto the street and headed for the basement. We went inside and I started feeling panicky again—I couldn't breathe, and my hands turned cold and sweaty.

The war had begun.

Explosions, noises, my heart beating loudly—I couldn't think through the fear and noise. Tears were welling up in my eyes—I was afraid for my loved ones and for myself.

Our basement wasn't built to be a bomb shelter. There were hot and cold pipes all over the place. A lot of dust. The ceiling was low. Tiny windows looked up onto the street level. Men stacked sandbags to block them so that no one would get hurt by flying shards of glass if there was a blast.

There were quite a few people down there.

After a while, once it all got quiet, I mustered up the courage to leave the basement and go outside. I took my phone out and turned on the news. People were gathering, talking loudly, trying to make sense of what was going on. But then . . . shelling: sharp and frequent. We bolted toward the shelter. A third panic attack, tears, more explosions than I could count . . .

Around noon. Our neighbor went to the shops to withdraw some cash from an ATM, but no such luck—there were Ukrainian fighters with machine guns there. But then there were more explosions and people started running back home. Terrified, our neighbor joined them. They said there were Ukrainian snipers positioned on the roofs of our neighboring apartment buildings in preparation for the invasion.

Hearing this, I called all of my friends to find out how they were doing. Some of their experiences had been very intense.

One of my classmates felt his building shake. Another had a bomb explode 100 yards from his house. Others felt their windows rattling.

And this is only the beginning of this hell.

Another school friend, Maryna, said it took her ages to get to a bomb shelter because the traffic was so terrible. Olha is holed up at home saying she's not going anywhere.

12:00 p.m. I persuaded Granny to go back home for a bit. We had a quick wash and lunch. I grabbed my diary because I want to start writing things down as they are happening.

I also took my laptop, paper, and pencils, in case I wanted to draw, a bit of food and some pillows and blankets. Then we went back to the basement.

3:20 p.m. We're hearing rumors that thirty minutes from now there will be planes, troops, and bombs.

4:00 p.m. Nothing's happened yet. Everyone's anxiously looking at each other.

I used to take sunny days for granted. A peaceful sky was nothing out of the ordinary. But it's all changed now. Before, when I'd hear about children being caught up in military combat, I never quite understood how terrible it was. I see it differently now that I've had to spend five hours holed up in a basement. I feel it clearly, with a sense of pain and dread. The world has changed for me; it has all new colors. The blue sky, bright sun, fresh air—it all seems so beautiful. I know now that we should rejoice in it all.

Every hour there's a new rumor on the news. One of them, which I believed at the time, made me think that keeping this diary might end up being a waste of time. It was a rumor that Russia had withdrawn its forces from Ukraine and Kharkiv had defended its independence. However, it was quickly proven false because we heard more explosions and shelling.

Right now, I have only one question on my mind: what will the night be like? I've been told that in wartime, nights and mornings are the most frightening because you never know what to expect. I guess we'll have to wait and see.

4:55 p.m. There's fighting. Machine-gun fire or missile launches? Unknown. We find a few sheets of cardboard from old boxes. We use them and the few blankets and pillows we grabbed earlier to make a sort of bed for us to sleep in. Someone had brought down a table and some chairs, and a few games to keep the children distracted.

The basement has two exits on either side leading out onto the street, but it's too scary to go outside. The basement runs under the entire length of our block, like a long tunnel. The men show us where the toilet is. Everyone understands that we'll be here a while.

The men are putting a lock on one of the doors so we can lock up at night. I decide to check if they'd also put a lock on the door at the other end of the basement, and it turned out they had not. Then, all of a sudden, my friend Nadya comes bursting through the doors as they were being shut by some of the grown-ups. She hugs me as tight as she can and I hug her back, trying to calm her down; she's shaking. She had heard explosions on the street.

6:40 p.m. It is dark now. I go outside for a breath of fresh air and it seems quiet. I return to the basement.

Nadya and her family think they'll go back home, but as they're getting ready to leave . . . *boom* . . . an explosion. . . . They decide to stay put after all.

The adults are all saying the worst is yet to come.

We're told that there is now a curfew—from 10 p.m. to 6 a.m. We're also told that no one is to leave the bomb

In the basement shelter the night of February 24, playing a game with some of the other children from the neighborhood.

shelter because shelling could start at any time. Yay . . . I doubt we'll get much sleep tonight.

9:00 p.m. I've never felt the time pass this slowly before. There's constant shelling. Apparently Russia has Ukraine surrounded. The Russians want Kharkiv to surrender. More shelling. I almost have another panic attack. I sit down next to Granny, and she hugs me. We're frightened. My neighbors are saying that the city might be forced to cut our water and electricity tomorrow, but we are not giving in to despair. All we can do is pray.

Everyone is minding their own business. Someone's sleeping (though I'm surprised they've managed that, so maybe they're just pretending). Others are talking to their friends and family over the phone, trying to figure out what to do next. One person is telling people about the latest news. Some of the older people are cowering in their chairs, not saying a word. We children are sitting around a table. Some are drawing, some playing cards, and I join a group playing dominoes. Others are just glued to their phones.

Granny's ringing her friends to see how they're doing. She's asking them if we could meet up and join them at a safer shelter, because we're too close to the action here and the shelling could get worse.

I'm not losing heart, because we're a cheerful lot and we support each other.

We're hearing that other countries are now proposing sanctions while refusing to send more weapons. In some ways, that might be for the best. . . .

Day 2

Fleeing for Safety

The rest of the night is quiet; there's no shelling. Everyone seems to be asleep. As for me, I start feeling drowsy around 10:30. I close my eyes and nod off.

I wake up at 6 a.m. Granny thinks it will be safe for us to run home again and grab a bite to eat, wash up, and then quickly come back down. We can't stay in our apartment for too long, because it's not safe up there on the fifth floor.

7:30 a.m. We leave the apartment. To my surprise, it starts snowing. They say it'll keep snowing for the next few days.

I try to walk like nothing is wrong, though we are afraid they'll start bombing again. But thankfully, it is a quiet morning. As we walk back to the basement, I scroll through the 180 messages sent to the school chat throughout the night.

One of my friends had been messaging to say he was scared he'd get blown up because he lived so close to the action. Another shared a video of what was happening in the city of Sumy, in the northeast. It looked like the city was on fire. Two of my classmates had stayed up messaging each other until midnight.

I have breakfast, a piece of buttered bread and some tea. I keep looking out the window to see if there are any tanks or missiles. There aren't.

8:00 a.m. We pack our things and go back outside. It's very cold. The word *shelter* had been written across the basement roof. I think, *Have they stopped bombing?* But then I hear an explosion: *No, they haven't.* We rush back down into the basement.

8:30 a.m. Next time I go outside I hear the sound of tanks driving by. They are headed in the direction of Kyiv. I think I see something flying through the sky at great speed. I guess that it must be a missile. Who knows if it hit or not. Maybe I'm just being paranoid.

8:40 a.m. I get a call from my classmate Maryna to tell me her aunt said the shelling will start up again in half an hour. Soon after the call, I fall asleep for about an hour. There isn't any shelling after all.

Then we learn that our Ukrainian tanks and APCs are stationed between apartment buildings. We're worried we'll end up being used as human shields. Granny decides she'll call her friend Inna and arrange for us to take a taxi to her home, which is on the other side of the city and farther from the action. We call the taxi company and wait for what feels like forever for them to get back to us.

The taxi finally arrives. We get in and set off. I ask Granny, "What about our things?"

She replies, "We have to leave them. Our lives are more important!"

I've left my friends.

That hurts. . . .

But we have to do what we have to do to survive. We have to save ourselves at any cost.

As we drive through Kharkiv, it seems strangely normal, apart from the long lines outside pharmacies and supermarkets.

There aren't any fighters near the shops now. While on the road, we see an army vehicle, but it's broken down. Then we see another one carrying Ukrainian fighters. "What on earth are they driving around here for?" I ask.

"It's not for you to worry about," I'm told.

9:10 a.m. After about 30 minutes, we arrive at Inna's house in New Bavaria, on the western edge of Kharkiv. It's a cute, cozy little house. There has still been some shelling here, but not much. This spot is a little higher up, so the explosions echo around more.

The kitchen is quite spacious, with a large dining table in the middle. The house has three bedrooms. We picked the one with a large fold-out couch for us to sleep on. It's a little cold, so we cover the window with a blanket. The house has a small wood burner near the front door. Out on the terrace, there is a hatch leading to an underground cellar.

In the kitchen, Inna has a huge seascape painting with some seashells glued to it. The painting isn't complete, though. Inna knows I can paint, so she suggests I finish it for her. I agree, because it feels like a good distraction from all the explosions we keep hearing in the distance. I also ask her to give me a little sheet of plywood because I've had an idea and want to paint an angel on it. I thought I'd try and paint it in the style of Gapchinska.

As for the situation back home, which I left barely an hour ago, it's best not to think about it.

My friend Rita and her mom heard from us that things in the city had quieted down a little, so they tried to drive to Pesochyn. They went to get their things but had no luck. The shelling had started up again, heavier than before. Fighters, tanks, bombs, explosions. It was too late for them to go. . . . Everyone was panicking and running toward the nearest basement. We aren't in as much danger as my friends are. What's going to happen next? Will they survive? Will our homes? No one can make any promises.

Huge bombs have been found on the streets of Kharkiv.

As for the rumors about cutting our water and electricity— thankfully those weren't true.

It's on the news that fighter planes have taken off from Kursk, but their destination is anyone's guess. There is one option, though—they're going to Kyiv, to the capital.

I've just realized that I left my phone charger in our basement in Kharkiv. My phone doesn't have much battery left. We don't have a lot of food left, either. Thankfully, Inna has a phone charger I can borrow, so at least we don't have to worry about that.

Messages keep coming in on the group chat. My friend Polyna texted me to say that there are tanks driving down Hvardiitsiv-Shyronintsiv Street, in the northeast of the city.

Painting an angel on the seascape artwork in Inna's kitchen in
New Bavaria, February 25, 2022.

I told Granny and Inna this, to which they just said, "There's nothing we can do about it."

We refuse to panic.

I've heard there are tanks firing just 200 yards away from my school. Myron, my schoolmate, left his basement to get some fresh air. Suddenly, there was a red light, the sound of a missile, and machine gunfire. He ran straight back to the basement. Dyana is holed up at her house in Velyka Danylivka, across the road from our neighborhood in northeast Kharkiv, watching things unfold.

My neighborhood, North Saltivka, is practically being erased. It is terrible! All the little streets I used to play in, the little courtyards, my favorite pizza place, and my school! It was all so beautiful! Such an awful shame . . . and for what? The tall block of apartment buildings at 60 Natalii Uzhvii Street was blown up by a missile. I saw that building—it was fine when we were on our way to Inna's. When I learned that it was destroyed, I got chills. New Bavaria, where we are now, is all quiet, but North Saltivka isn't. The school announced a two-week holiday. Yay . . . doesn't sound like much of a holiday. . . .

And now for some lighter news. We got the little wood burner going, and it's my job to tend the fire. I keep telling myself it's important to look for the positive, no matter how bad it gets. For now, I'll just enjoy watching the firewood burning in the furnace. We sit around it to keep each other company. It's not so scary when we're together.

I get curious about what the cellar we'll be hiding in is like. I open the hatch and go down two steps. There's another hatch in front of me, so I unfasten that too. Beyond that is a very deep cellar. I have no doubt that we will be safe here.

7:00 p.m. It's started getting dark outside. There has been some shelling. We wonder whether it's our cue to go hide in the cellar. . . .

7:15 p.m. The explosions are getting louder. We suspect they'll start using the Grad systems, and those are not known for their precision. They're bombing hard around Velyka Danylivka where my friend Tolya lives. I hope he's staying strong.

Inna's listening to the explosions and trying to figure out where they land. She's trying to calm Granny down by telling her that they sound far away.

After dinner the atmosphere feels more relaxed. We are talking. I'm watching YouTube videos about Minecraft. The government is telling people to take up arms and join the fight.

7:50 p.m. It's very dark out. The darkest kind of dark. I feel too scared to go outside. Inna's friend has come over so we can all keep each other company.

We're not turning on the news because it just frightens us. With the heat from the little wood furnace, I'm feeling sleepier by the second. I can still feel my heart beating anxiously but I'm trying to calm myself. Once the fire in the furnace is out, Inna calls me into the living room where it's warmer. I sit down on a comfy armchair and recline it. It's warm in there. I wind down a little and, for a moment, forget all about the horrors I'd been through over the past couple of days.

We say a prayer together and then Inna goes to bed.

9:00 p.m. Everything is silent. We're hoping for a quiet night, just like the one before it. . . .

It's now around 10 p.m. I can barely keep my eyes open anymore. I don't think it will be long before I'm fast asleep. . . .

Day 3

A Restless Evening

7:40 a.m. I wake up. In terms of shelling, there isn't much of it, and it's far away.

I'm leaning against a wall and I feel it shake. That's terrifying. "They are bombing Zmyiv," Inna says.

8:00 a.m. Inna's gone out to the store.

She comes back two hours later. Food prices have gone up and everything's expensive now. Some things aren't even available anymore. The shop had a fresh delivery of bread, but there isn't enough for everyone. She says everyone is buying vodka.

I'm starting to believe that we were right to leave our apartment behind yesterday, unlike my friend Rita and her mom. Our lives are more important than a few bits of clothing or even the apartment itself. It doesn't matter if you haven't got your things or that you've left your home behind. You'll come back one day. Unfortunately, not everyone understands that. . . . With each day, I'm learning that life goes on—even in wartime. We hang onto the hope that sooner or later, the war will be over.

Right now, they're bombing our airport. That's quite far away from here, but we can hear it very clearly. If I can hear it here, in New Bavaria, then I can't imagine what it would sound like if I were closer to it all. And also, I can't help but wonder how many years will it take to build it all back up again. Who knows? Apparently, the first two days of a war are the hardest, but we're on day three now.

Last night we thought we heard some Ukrainian army vehicles driving by for the first time here.

I saw this post by Oleksii Potapenko on his Instagram stories. I'd call it a cri de coeur:

> *Why aren't any of the Ukrainian networks showing the sheer hell unfolding in Schastia (Luhansk Oblast)—the people there are living in ruins!*
>
> *Ukrainian civilians must be evacuated urgently! Why is no one saying anything? Why isn't anyone doing anything? How can you treat your own people this way? As many people as possible must be told about this so that everyone can start doing something! Helping with the evacuation—anything!*

We were told that the explosions we heard yesterday were from the city beltway getting shelled. Ukrainian tanks destroyed the Russian tanks near Pesochyn and Vysokyi village. Pesochyn has a road that leads to Kyiv, and Vysokyi leads to Dnipro. The Russian tanks were headed to Kyiv, but our tanks stopped them. . . .

1:00 p.m. There's a big round of explosions. They're not as loud, but it's frightening nonetheless. They changed the curfew again—it's now from 6 p.m. to 6 a.m.

They're saying on the news that the Russians have already suffered three thousand casualties, but that Russian networks aren't mentioning that.

I was thinking about what a beautiful city Kharkiv is . . . or was. How much time and money were spent to create a place so perfect, but then, in an instant, it was all blown to hell! They're shelling civilians more than they did at the start of the war.

Granddad told us he's been walking around the streets. We're shocked—there's a war going on and he thought he'd just take a stroll!

Tolya's situation back in Velyka Danylivka is getting worse. The bombing there is even heavier. Myron, Dad's friend, has a missile lying in the courtyard of his building. I'm scared. We can still hear the explosions, but they're far away.

Sveta and Rita decided to take a train to Bezliudivka. As I write this, they're down in the Prospekt Haharina metro station. Apparently there are a lot of people there. As they were going down to the station, there was a hail of missiles behind them. Thankfully, no one was hurt.

As for our neighborhood back home, friends say that the buildings are shaking. . . . My heart is full of fear. What will happen next is anyone's guess.

3.10 p.m. There's heavy shelling now. We've tidied up the cellar in case we need to stay here a while. Around me, there are crates of glass jars, full of all sorts of stuff. Pickled tomatoes and cucumbers, as well as raspberry and apricot jam. Granny and Inna bring in a bench, and I throw some coats over it. The walls are rounded. It's quite a small room so it's not too cold in here. We climb back up to the house.

3:55 p.m. Two sudden explosions about five miles away. We immediately run to the cellar. Quiet again now. Down in the cellar, we said a prayer and sent it on. Fear engulfs us. We're hoping and praying—that's just about all we can do.

The sun's going down. We want peace. We can't remember our old dreams anymore, or all the things we thought were important. We can't recall our old arguments or troubles. All of those past concerns just don't compare. When there's a war going on, you've only got one goal—to stay alive. Everything that seemed hard or bad in the past becomes trivial. You're afraid for the lives of your loved ones, and every day is interrupted by the sound *BOOM*. . . . You start thinking about how fortunate you are that this one rocket hit far away from you, while hiding the terror gripping your heart. You pray all day, asking God for peace. You hold on to every minute, every second of your life. . . .

We keep calling all of our friends to check up on them, and we realize that the Russians are shelling all over Ukraine. The news is now saying there is a full-scale war going on. The words *full-scale* are frightening. They put fear into your soul and across the entire country. My soul is screaming. I'm hurting, but I must carry on, stay safe, and hope that the war will be over soon and we will have peace. I want to take something to calm my nerves, but more than that, I wish this was all just a terrible nightmare I could wake up from.

5:40 p.m. It's dark outside. We get a call from Granny's friend Nelya. She says there's a Ukrainian tank stationed just outside a nearby kindergarten and that it keeps shooting at something. Then we get a call from my teacher at school. She shares a terrifying story with us: "A nearby garage caught fire. We were holed up in the basement of another garage ourselves, so we realized we weren't safe there anymore. We decided to run over to the school basement. As we were running, there were missiles flying just above us. We ran for our lives. Thankfully, we managed to get there without anybody getting hurt."

I was very scared for her. She's my favorite teacher.

6:57 p.m. Inna made *zapekanka* for supper, and we had it with some raspberry jam and mint tea. I calmed down a little, but then there were more explosions. We were told it was our guys shooting toward Russia from their positions on the city beltway. There is constant noise from all the planes and missiles. This time last night it was all quiet, but tonight, it's deafening.

Apparently a group of saboteurs were caught in Kharkiv. They were trying to rig the streets of Kharkiv with explosives.

As I write tonight, I don't feel much hope.

Once the shelling died down, Inna called me into her room. It was small space with a single window, but it was the safest room in the house. She turned on a little yellow night-light. The rest of the lights in the house were turned off to keep the planes from spotting them. I prayed things would stay quiet until morning.

At that very moment, they started bombing the beltway and there were planes flying around. I tried my best to stay calm, but ended up having a little panic attack after all—I was struggling to breathe and I felt like my chest was being crushed.

They were bombing, we were sitting. I thought it would be safer if I lay down. Even though the shelling was far away, Granny spotted a searchlight from the window and insisted on going to the cellar. I went with her. Inna refused to join us because it had become quiet and she was worried that if the house were to collapse from an explosion, we would be trapped without anyone knowing we were down there.

7:00 p.m. We're down in the cellar, having some tea. I called out to Inna to fetch my notebook so that I can write things down as they're happening. Things are letting up and I'm starting to relax a bit.

By the way, Rita and her mom made it to the train, and now they're safe.

I'm sitting in the cellar, writing in my book using the little light on the phone. North Saltivka is being showered with rockets.

After a while, we leave the cellar. It's all quiet—heaven for my ears.

We spend some time in Inna's room, but then we go to bed.

Day 4

Hell in My Old Neighborhood

I slept, waking up at 8 a.m. This seems late for me now. I rolled over and the bright sun was shining on me. A beam of light illuminated my face. To me, it seemed like a beautiful day. I wanted to go outside and enjoy the sunshine. But then I immediately remembered.

It turned out that there was especially heavy bombing last night, far away from here, though. I was fast asleep as it was happening. I was just so tired of listening to all the explosions that I must have simply switched off. Velyka Danylivka was on fire. North Saltivka was being shelled by Grads. This was the first time in three days that there was shelling late at night. I got in touch with my friend Olha. She told me what has been happening to her. The kindergarten had its roof blown off. A nearby building entrance was destroyed in a blast, and a man and a woman got hit in the back with debris. The ambulance took a long time (an hour) to get there, and kept refusing to take them, but did so in the end.

Olha was in line outside the Equator Mall, but just as she was approaching the till, the electricity was cut. She didn't get her shopping done, but she'll try again today.

10:00 a.m. We've run out of water, so we decided to go to the spring. It seemed like the street was totally empty, but we did

31

meet a couple of people. There were explosions, but they were far away. We brought back some water. Inna was showing me around her garden. She had orchard trees growing there, a raspberry bush, and a blackcurrant bush. There was also a strawberry patch. She was showing me where she was going to plant some flowers, but then . . . *BOOM!* . . . Two explosions very close by! We ran to the cellar, though Inna stayed upstairs.

Granddad Yosip took a picture of a terrible scene he witnessed and sent it to us. There was a bomb lying on the road right in front of a shop. The bomb was like two yards long. The bomb isn't armed, it's only a marker. There are Russian tanks over in the city center. We climbed out of the cellar, but fifteen minutes later I went back down again because there were more sounds.

We are very lucky with our neighbors here; they take care of us and we take care of them. They bring us food. We climbed down into the cellar several times throughout the day.

6:00 p.m. It's completely dark outside. With every day that passes I start hating the night more and more. I don't want the sun to disappear below the horizon but, sadly, that's not in my control. Evenings are full of the unknown and engulf me in fear.

9:30 p.m. It's all quiet where we are and I feel calmer. I'm grateful to my classmate Kyrylo! He keeps posting silly videos in the school chat, recording himself making faces using funny camera filters on his phone. I've been laughing so hard I almost fell out of bed and my belly hurts.

Day 5

An Unexpected Start

I woke up at 3 a.m. I was just dropping back off when fighter jets started dropping bombs. I can feel the anxiety taking over. Every explosion brings a chill through my body. Inna called for us to climb down to the cellar and said she would join us this time. We got down there and stayed put. I can't imagine how dangerous it must be outside if Inna decided to come with us. I drifted off down there. The curfew's been changed again: 3 p.m. to 6 a.m.

8:00 a.m. More shelling, but it seems to be far away.

Granny's friend rang us and said a house in Vysokyi village has been destroyed, but there were no casualties apart from a dog. Turns out that was what all the shelling we just heard was.

Later, Granny and Inna tried going to the shops to get some food, but it didn't work out. Granny said, "I was standing in the line and I was very frightened. There was more bombing around us than when we went to get water yesterday. People are still lining up for food, having gotten used to all the shelling. People are prepared to wait in line amid all the shelling just to get a morsel of food."

We heard from Granny Zyna. She said that she wanted to break curfew yesterday to go to the pharmacy. She asked

Granddad Yosip to go with her, but he said the nearest one was closed. She suggested they go over to another on Heroiv Pratsi. I feel like, if her house were being bombed, she'd be as calm as a boa. He refused, because the curfew was very strict and it wasn't safe to go outside. Why the hell are they shelling people who are just trying to buy their medicine?

Today, negotiations were held between delegations from both the Russian Federation and Ukraine. A block of apartment buildings was destroyed this afternoon. There are casualties. Accidents. The bodies aren't taken away. Civilians are being shelled from every direction.

There's a parking lot next to Granny Iryna's building, and the buildings behind it were hit in the shelling.

6:00 p.m. It's dark now. I'm starting to hate the night even more and it grows with every passing day.

Day 6

Our Apartment Is Gone

I had a wonderful dream last night. I dreamt of my school . . . and, most importantly, of a peaceful sky. My friends and I were running around, carefree. It felt like the good old days. . . . I wish things weren't the way they are now. I'm so tired of the sound of explosions; I really want to hear the sounds of peacetime again—birds singing and the sound of rain. It was so nice before the war. . . I want to go back to my old life.

The shelling around 6 a.m. this morning was no joke, but it's quiet now, I think. Even so, the grown-ups are lining the windows with Scotch tape in case of a blast.

There are planes flying around. In the city center, Freedom Square was just destroyed by a single missile strike. There's a video of the bomb exploding. In it, you can see two cars, one of which swerves to the side. Some people jump out of it. Two more people run away from the impact site. They're saying that bombs also hit the zoo, Derzhprom, Gorky Park, the university, and the opera house, as well as the Philharmonic.

Everything is happening at such incredible speed.

10:00 a.m. Inna went to buy some groceries, despite shelling hailing down, and this time she was successful.

12:00 p.m. We have heard some traumatizing news. We got a call from one of our neighbors, telling us that our old kitchen has been hit by missile.

We're told there are emergency services outside our block of buildings. Granny is on the phone trying to get someone to pick up the keys from here, but no one can help.

As for the kind of missile that caused all this, the emergency workers are saying that it was a submunition from a cluster bomb (which are banned under the Geneva Convention). They urgently need to get inside to check that there aren't any unexploded submunitions threatening to level the entire building. They had to break into the apartment. There weren't any unexploded submunitions, but the kitchen was blown to pieces and the hallway is full of debris.

This hurts, because my childhood was spent there. Attacking my home is the same as attacking a piece of me. I'm starting to feel depressed, but I'm fighting it with food. I feel like my heart has been squashed.

There were such memories there! Our Italian furniture, our fancy dinner sets, the glass table. All those memories blown to bits. Tears are streaming down my face, and that's only a fraction of my sorrow. I don't care as much about the things themselves as much as I do the memories they held. I spent my childhood there, and it has simply been destroyed!

There isn't much left of the apartment. Why doesn't anyone care? Why? Do you enjoy fighting in cities, destroying everything in your wake, instead of fighting in the battlefields? Kharkiv is being destroyed bit by bit.

Photographs of the horrible destruction in our apartment; the kitchen (top) and my room (bottom).

If you want a detailed description of what happened to my apartment, then read on—we've been given all the details. . . .

The balcony, the kitchen, and the part of the hallway leading into it were all destroyed. Bits of plaster, rubble, and broken glass fill the hallway. My bedroom windows were blown off, but the room itself seems intact. The living room, along with its windows, was spared. The front door was so bashed up that even if Granny had managed to get the key over there, it wouldn't have helped. The emergency workers closed the front door as best they could and fixed it in place with tape. We want to weld the door shut. Will there be anything left in our apartment after the war?

7:00 p.m. Today has been a day of constant aviation. As usual, once it got dark outside, Inna's friend went back home. Granny was in the kitchen making tea when, suddenly, she saw a giant drone. All of its lights were flashing, and it flew so low over the house that she dropped to the floor. Inna and I were in her little room when we heard it. It sounded strange, not like a plane at first. We got down on the floor. We didn't rush down to the cellar this time, because if the house were blown up, no one would know that we were down there. We would just get buried. The drone did a circle around the area, dropping bombs as it went. Rivers of tears. I lay on the bed, and for the first time in my life, I just thought about how I really want to live. My heart stops every time another bomb gets dropped. I was holding on to every minute, every second. I've never been this close to death. I was praying for the plane to fly away and for the bombs not to hit the house, just praying *God, help me*. I couldn't breathe. After a while it all got quiet, and I eventually settled down.

I checked my phone, and Evhen was on his way to Poltava when he sent a photo he'd taken of a flying missile.

Dyana was leaving Velyka Danylivka and there were houses burning behind her. We went down to the cellar after all. I tried to get some rest down there, but I couldn't sleep, so we ended up going back upstairs.

Day 7

We're Leaving Kharkiv

I had a dream. We're in our Toyota, driving down to our bombed-out apartment. We go in, and the hallway is filled with garbage. We go into the kitchen and find that the cupboards are undamaged. The table is broken. I start filming it. Suddenly, there is a missile flying toward the neighboring building. I can't talk. That's where the dream ended.

There was artillery fire this morning.

The Internet was cut off at 6 a.m.

Because of the air raids, people are starting to panic-buy, emptying the shops of food.

Granny and I want to leave Kharkiv for Western Ukraine, farther from the border. We called everyone we know to figure out how we could do this. They're saying we should stay put for now. Many of my schoolmates are going to Dnipro or Poltava first, and on to Western Ukraine from there.

Inna saw many cars leaving the city. They had the word *Children* written on every side.

They're saying that the trains evacuating people have had the seats taken out. Thirty to forty hours standing up. We decided we'd stay in Kharkiv for now.

But then, after thinking it through, we realized that we should go to Lviv, because there's a scary rumor that the Russians could start purging Kharkiv of all resistance by obliterating it with bombs in a few days. I spent half the day trying to call a taxi company, but every time they picked up, we'd get cut off. Mom kept sending us phone numbers for drivers in Kharkiv, but none of them were picking up. I did get through to someone who agreed to take us to the train station, but he could only do it in a couple of days. Another company picked up, but we got cut off again. I sent more messages to Mom and Dad, asking for help, but they're not going through.

I fell into a depression. All I could think was *We are doomed, I'm scared.* I'd stopped talking and my face felt like it would never smile again. Then I thought I'd get back to painting my Gapchinska angel, which made me feel better. I'm not losing hope. I keep praying that we'll leave for Lviv or even get out of the country. We shall do, and shall continue doing, everything we possibly can. We're under curfew right now, so we can't go to the Southern Train Station.

We kept hoping and praying to leave this city. But then, suddenly, we had a bit of luck. Inna's daughter, Lukyia, sent us the phone numbers for two Red Cross volunteers. We only managed to reach one of them, who agreed to pick us up in fifteen minutes and take us to Dnipro, about 140 miles southwest, where Inna's family lives. Oh joy! We gathered our things and went to stand on the street to wait for the car. I had to leave my painting of the angel behind. Pity. I never got to finish a part of its dress. At first, Inna said she didn't want to come with us to Dnipro and only came along to see us off, but when she saw the smoke from all the shelling, she changed her mind. She ran back into the house to look for her passport and told us not to

41

wait for her. She didn't want us to miss our ride. Granny and I heard the sound of explosions. We didn't know if the car would be able to find its way to us or not. We were very nervous and kept asking God for help. We got a call from the volunteers, Todor and Oleh, but Inna was still in the house. I didn't know how to give them directions, but then I saw a Volkswagen with a red cross on it and I knew it was them. We got in the car at 4:50 p.m. Granny asked them to go around the corner so that we could say goodbye to Inna, but then there she was, running toward us. She decided to go with us to Dnipro after all! She didn't take anything with her, just her passport, which is what she'd run back for. We set off. We passed twelve checkpoints on our way. As we got closer to Dnipro, there was a huge line of cars, several miles long, trying to get into the city. It got dark and started raining. We entered the city. It was quiet there, so my ears were happy. The buildings were undamaged. A peaceful sky—what else could you ask for?

We thanked Todor and Oleh for taking us to a safe place. They said there was no need to pay them, and we said our goodbyes.

We met up with Inna's family. I felt happy. There was a beautiful park just across the road behind us. We went into the apartment and told everyone about what we'd been through. It took me a while to relax.

We still want to get to Western Ukraine, but we'll think about that tomorrow. For now, we just want to enjoy a peaceful night here with Inna's family.

Day 8

Awful News

I woke up. I thought the night had been uneventful, but it turns out there had been some shelling somewhere far in the distance.

Granny got a text from one of her friends saying that her husband has been killed. He had gone to fetch some water from a spring, and then *BANG*, a cluster bomb. The bomb fragments had cut his entire body. His leg got blown off. He was forty-seven. He was a good man and a caring father. We had spoken to him only a few days ago, and today he's gone. It's terrifying. We are in shock.

11:00 a.m. We needed to withdraw some cash and get some groceries. I agreed to go.

When I got back, I learned that we're going to go to the train station to catch a train to Western Ukraine.

Our hosts called us a taxi. We didn't have to wait too long for it to come. We said our farewells. Inna is staying behind with her family. She told us that everything would be all right. We hope to see each other again. She also said that I should come back and finish my angel painting. Perhaps one day, after the war. We wished each other good luck. We got in the taxi and got talking to the driver—he told us he's from Donetsk. We asked what the fare was, and he said it was free. The people in this city are so nice.

Granny and I arrived at the train station. We went inside and tried to find out what to do next, but no one seemed to know anything.

Suddenly, there was an announcement: "Warning. Air raid. Take cover." We rushed down into the subway connecting the platforms. While we were there, Granny asked a young lady what we should do. The lady was a volunteer called Rada. She said she could help us.

We found out that there was a train going to Truskavets (near Lviv) at 2 p.m., so we decided to try to catch it.

The air raid siren eventually stopped. Rada took us to the waiting room. There were some other people there who we tried to talk to about what we'd been through, but they were locals, so it was hard for them to understand how bad things have been in Kharkiv.

1:00 p.m. We had some tea and cookies. At 1 p.m., we thought we'd better start getting ready because the train would be arriving soon.

At last, our train's arrival was announced. We ran, along with a large crowd of others, toward the platform. We got out onto the platform and tried to make our way to our car. It wasn't easy, but we made it. Yay!

I was sitting on the window ledge, waiting for the train to start moving and for the crowd to shrink down as people filtered onto the train. The train shook as it started moving. The people left behind on the platform all started running

Bombed apartment buildings photographed on our way out of Kharkiv to Dnipro.

somewhere else. They'd missed it. But the train was moving, and we were on our way!

The conductor came by and told me to climb up to the top bunk, which I happily did. The trip was long but fun. I made friends with Lera and we spent half the day laughing. She's from Kharkiv and we're the same age too, so we understand each other.

6:00 p.m. The sun is setting. . . . I'm trying to imagine what it's like where we're going, but I can't.

It's dark outside. Lera was saying how beautiful the weeds out the window look, which really made me laugh. I suppose some people have to figure out where they're going and what to do next, but others might as well just admire the weeds. Ha!

There were some scary moments during our trip. The train kept slowing down, and sometimes it stopped altogether. The lights in the car kept going out. Every time the lights would come back on, everyone would breathe a sigh of relief. There were times when I was too scared to speak. Later, Granny told me she'd seen explosions in the distance, but she didn't tell me about them so as not to frighten me further. I guess that's why the train was stopping—they were waiting for a signal that it was safe to keep going.

We passed by Kyiv. That was frightening too.

Relieved to be on the train to Dnipro.

Day 9

A Meeting That Would Change Our Lives

I woke up at six in the morning. We found out that the train is now terminating at Uzhhorod. I looked at the map and saw that Uzhhorod is in the far western end of Ukraine. At first, we thought we'd go there. But once we learned that we could go to Romania or Germany with my new friend Lera, we thought, *Why not got with them?* But then we realized it would be easier to stay on the train, because if we went to Lviv, we'd have to wait for three hours to get on a bus to get to the Romanian border, and it was unclear what would happen once we got there. So we settled on staying onboard until the end after all.

Lera and her mother got off the train in Lviv. We said good-bye, hoping we'd one day meet in Kharkiv. We're headed toward Uzhhorod, where there's a border with Slovakia and Hungary. We'll figure out the rest when we get there.

8:00 a.m. A lot of people got off at Lviv, so our car was half empty. We moved to a different compartment where there was an empty bottom bunk.

A train conductor came up to us. She was from Zaporizhzhia, and she told us that earlier the Russian occupiers seized the Zaporizhzhia Nuclear Power Plant. Its nuclear reactor is ten times more powerful than the one at the Chernobyl plant. If it explodes, it will destroy everything in its path. And beyond.

1:00 p.m. It's been five hours, and the trip is long and boring, and now we're in Mukachevo. I can see Mukachevo Castle. I took a picture of it. I remember coming here last summer, but this time I'm trying to escape a war. We arrived in Uzhhorod. The first thing we did was go to have something to eat at the station. Then we were taken onto a bus. We're driving, but we don't know to where. No one knows what's in store for us. I'm realizing that we've become refugees. Perhaps we will have the chance to go to the UK or the EU and live there.

We arrived at the office for registration and placement. We were given a document with an address on it, and some volunteers drove us there in their car.

We arrived at the address. It's a school. We went inside. There was a man walking just behind us. He said hello in what I first thought was German but then realized was actually English. He wanted to ask me something, but I apologized and said I couldn't talk right now. I didn't know what was going on.

We were greeted by Myna. She's in charge here. As she was showing us around the school, the man from before started filming us.

I didn't know what to do with myself. I could feel the tension inside me, and the stress of the situation was over-whelming. I had to find something to do. I needed to figure out where I was, what I was, what was going on in the world.

How am I supposed to sleep on a mattress in a school gym instead of in my warm cozy bed? Where am I going to wash? There's no hot bath here. I want to go back to school—my school—to my friends. I feel numb.

While I was walking around, trying to occupy myself, Granny told the man who was filming us that I was writing a book. (How she managed that when he doesn't speak any Russian is a mystery to me. . . .) That caught his attention. I came over and said hello. His name is Flavian. He works for Channel 4, a British TV channel.

I told him about everything that has happened to me. He asked if he could interview me on camera.

While they were looking for a room to film the interview in, Flavian and I got talking and I learned that he's French. They couldn't find a room after all, so we decided to do the interview right there in the middle of the school hall. During the interview, Flavian operated the camera. I read him my book. After that, Paraic, an Irish reporter working for Channel 4, asked me some questions.

We asked them if they could help us leave the country or find somewhere to live. They said they'd see if there was anything they could do. I'm hoping there is.

There were about fifty other people staying at this school gym. I was shown my bed and went to sleep.

Day 10

I Miss Kharkiv

I wasn't myself yesterday, but I've woken up feeling a bit better.

The situation in Kharkiv is very bad. It's hard to understand what's going on. The Ukrainian army asked some of our friends to leave the basement of their apartment buildings because it wasn't safe there. They were put on trucks. Where are they taking them? No one knows. Down to the city center, perhaps. . . .

Half of Granny's friend's building has been demolished. All our friends still there want to leave Kharkiv. They've finally realized it's not safe in that city. But it's harder to get out now.

Some of our friends and neighbors were taken to some street somewhere and just abandoned there, literally in the middle of the road.

I phoned Olha. She's in Dnipro now. Apparently, it's all quiet there.

2:00 p.m. The reporters came back. I talked to them and then translated for Granny. We told them our story of the first few days of the war.

We went down to the city center for a look around.

Every building, every landmark, reminded me of Kharkiv. It pained my soul to think of Kharkiv as I saw the bridges overlooking the beautiful views of the city. Kharkiv is, or was, a lot prettier than Uzhhorod. But the chocolate here is still good. We bought a new phone charger now that I can't borrow Inna's anymore.

When we got back to the school I felt miserable, but I'm trying not to lose heart.

Day 11

A Sunny Day

It was an uneventful morning. We woke up, got ourselves ready, and went back down to the city center for a walk. I'm falling in love with this city. I especially like the promenade along the Uzh River!

We were enjoying our day. I called my school friend Khrystyna. We spent about half an hour chatting. Then I got a text from Paraic. They wanted to make a short movie about us. I sent them our location.

After a while, we met up with the reporters. We were filming something for Channel 4 News in the UK. They asked me to call one of my friends. I thought I'd call Olha, but she wasn't picking up. However . . .

I had already spoken to Khrystyna today, so I thought, *Why not? Why not record an interview with her?* I asked her mom for permission and then we started recording.

Khrystyna is in Kharkiv. She's so fearless, being there. She was talking about what she does when there's shelling. She and her family all go to their hallway and wait it out. At times, I acted as a translator for her.

Once we were done filming, we went back to the school.

Day 12

Getting a New Passport Is Impossible

We've been talking about what we should do. We can't stay here, because the school will be starting soon and there's nowhere available to rent here. We've decided we need to leave Ukraine altogether. But to do that, we need to get Granny a new passport because her old one was left back at our bombed apartment.

We paid a visit to the Sovyne Hnizdo (the registration center). We were taken to the passport department, but it had been turned into a makeshift hospital for COVID patients. We met someone who helped us get through to the help hotline, but they told us they're not taking on any new cases until the end of the war. Yeah. . . . So that's the situation, but we're determined we'll find a way into another country.

We went back to the town. Back in Dnipro, we had withdrawn quite a bit of cash from an ATM. But we'd discovered that there weren't any apartments available to rent here, so we didn't have anything to spend it on. We wanted to put it back in the bank, but no such luck. The banks here weren't accepting Ukrainian currency for some reason, so we decided to exchange our hryvnia into more stable euros, but the rate wasn't very good. I can buy 1 euro for 43 hryvnia, and sell 1 euro for 38 hryvnia. A euro used to cost about 30 hryvnia, and the difference between buying and selling was never more than 1 hryvnia, if that.

We returned to the school. The reporters called their colleague Nik and introduced us. I was telling her that I had no idea what we should do next. Should we stay in Ukraine or leave?

Before the phone call, an entertainer came to the school, dressed as a polar bear.

There was music, and all the children danced.

HUNGARY

"Ukraine's Refugee Crisis Is Unprecedented.
The Response Must Be, Too."

—*The New York Times*, March 15, 2022

Day 13

Our New Life Awaits

8:30 a.m. Soon after I woke up, we decided that we are definitely going to go to Hungary.

We called Father Emilio, a Catholic priest in Uzhhorod. We were given his contact details by the reporters. Father Emilio gave us the number for a volunteer. We then called the volunteer, who agreed that he would come pick us up at the school and take us to Chop, Ukraine, near the Hungarian border. And from there, we'll cross the border to Záhony.

"What time does the train leave?" we asked him.

"10:25," he replied.

"Will we get there on time?"

He told us not to worry—it would only take us half an hour.

We got ready to leave. I ran back and forth around the school like a rocket, trying to gather up our things. We rang the volunteer again, and he said he'd be there in fifteen minutes.

Granny and I said goodbye to Myna and thanked her for the warm welcome. Our car arrived. We introduced ourselves to the volunteer. His name is Arsenyi. He drove us all the way to the train station in Chop. We shared our story with him. Around this time, I called the TV reporters. They were waiting for us in Záhony.

10:00 a.m. We arrived. Arsenyi helped us find our way around the train station. He also helped get us our tickets. I was filming everything. We joined a large line. The train was late for some reason. The line was for border control. We were supposed to leave at 10:25 a.m., but it was 12 p.m. by the time we were cleared to depart.

Granny and I presented our papers to the officials, but . . . we needed one more document—a consent form for me to leave the country, signed by a parent.

We'd had a serious row with Mom about this before she left for Turkey. There was already talk of war in Ukraine, but she was convinced that there wouldn't be an invasion. Getting that permit costs money, and she didn't want to spend hers on something she thought we wouldn't need.

We were stopped. They were trying to decide whether they could let us through into Hungary. We stood there, tears in our eyes, praying. *Please let us through.* And they did! They said that even though we didn't have a consent document from Mom, and even though Granny didn't have her passport, they would let us through because normal rules don't apply during wartime. They let us pass, thanks to our prayers and our strong faith in God. I was overjoyed.

We got on the train. Hooray! Granny found a seat and I stood up. After just twenty minutes, we were in Záhony. We waited for them to let us off the train. They were checking the passports of every single person on board. I was afraid they'd ask for that consent form again. Through the window, I saw the TV reporters on the platform. I waved at them and they spotted me. When we were making our way slowly toward the train doors to get off, I saw Flavian casually climb down straight onto the tracks and start filming. That was funny.

After about forty-five minutes, it was finally our turn. They checked our papers and we got off the train. Thank goodness they didn't ask for the consent form.

We met up with the reporters, then were sent to the registration point. Unfortunately, the reporters weren't allowed in. Once Granny got her visa—valid for three months—we found them again. We immediately got our tickets, which some lady was handing out as if they were flyers, and then we all ran straight to the train headed for Budapest—the capital of Hungary.

All this time, my schoolmates were continuing to send messages in the school chat. Everyone from my year at school is leaving Ukraine now. Polyna fled to Germany, Maryna went to Kremenchuk, Central Ukraine. And Kyrylo is at the Polish border.

No one speaks any English or Russian in Hungary. Maybe a few police and volunteers, but apart from that, it seems to be Hungarian only.

We're about to arrive in Budapest. At first when I was looking at the city through the train window, it seemed ordinary and primitive. I was quickly proven wrong. . . . The train stopped at a platform just outside the station building. We disembarked and I was shocked by what I saw. Keleti is a beautiful train station with giant columns propping up the enormous glass roof. The reporters began filming me. I went inside the main station building and there were statues along the walls. The volunteers were handing out food, water, toiletries—anything you could ask for.

I left the train station and had a look around. It was incredible! I won't stop saying it—what a beautiful city! A big shopping center, old buildings, the commotion of people and cars all around me. I couldn't contain my emotions. I'm in Europe! For the first time ever!

We had to cross the road twice to wait for the reporter's car, and each time Granny and Paraic kept having to wait on the island in the middle of the road because they couldn't keep up. That was funny.

We were picked up by Piotr, their driver, who is originally from Poland, and our reporters went to a hotel. We said goodbye to them and agreed to meet again tomorrow. And Piotr took us to someone who had agreed to let us stay with them at their apartment for a short time.

We drove to the other side of the city. Some of the streets here reminded me of Kharkiv. Old temples. We were approaching the Széchenyi Chain Bridge and it was beautiful there. The river was enchanting. A boat with bright lights all over it, streetlights that gave the river a romantic feel. There were incredible buildings on either side of the river: Buda Castle, the Hungarian Parliament, and many other interesting things. I was speechless. I just kept saying, "This is all so European!"

Piotr told us how the city got its name. According to him, Pest is named because of all the grocers there. And Buda is called that because there's a castle on that side of the river.

8:00 p.m. We arrived and met up with our new host. His name is Attila, and he was happy to see us. He showed us around our room, the shower, and the kitchen, and said that we were free to use all of the rooms and that we'd talk more tomorrow. That's how nice he was to us.

I think we've got a big day ahead of us tomorrow, but today, I dropped from exhaustion.

Day 14

A Special Evening

I woke up at half past eight. This is the first time I've slept through the entire night since the invasion began. I dozed with a smile on my face, thinking of yesterday.

I told Attila about what happened in Kharkiv and how we ended up here.

Today we want to explore our new surroundings. And by the way, we're staying close to the city center. The building we're in has a curious layout. The front door of the apartment opens up to an atrium overlooking a small courtyard. Attila took a few pictures of us just now. He's a photographer.

The reporters introduced me through the phone to Delara and Tom—their colleagues from Channel 4 News. We are going to meet up. I can't wait!

Time passed. I walked around the flat impatiently, looking forward to meeting them. And then someone rang the buzzer. It was them. I hurried to let them in and immediately got lost! Eventually, after a few minutes, I found the front door. We introduced ourselves. I took them up to the apartment. We started talking and I told them my story, starting from the very beginning. After a while, we were joined by the other Channel 4 News reporters. I went to let them in and I didn't get lost this time. We recorded an interview. They are all going on to Moldova, but we're staying here with Delara and Tom. Oh well . . . pity. I wished them a safe journey. I'm really going to miss them.

After they left, Granny and I decided to go for a walk down by the river. I grabbed a map and we set off. However, we weren't quite sure how to get there. We asked a Hungarian girl, but she spoke very little English. I explained everything to her using a translator app, and she gave us directions, but we could barely understand her. Then, as we kept walking, we asked some other people, but they didn't even look our way. This is some kind of discrimination!

We went for a walk around the park next to our apartment instead. Afterward, we wanted to find a pharmacy. Thank God we met another girl who spoke English. She took us to the "chemist," but it turned out to be a medical laboratory instead of a pharmacy. She tried giving us new directions, but we couldn't really make sense of them. I forgot to say that the sirens on ambulances, fire trucks, and police cars here in Budapest are very loud. They could turn it down a little!

That's when I got a call from Delara inviting us on a riverboat tour to do some sightseeing. We were delighted! We accepted her invitation without hesitation. They'll be picking us up at 7:45 p.m., and we'll go on a boat to get a better look at Budapest.

7:46 p.m. The doorbell rang. I ran to the door, tripping over myself. We got into a taxi. We drove through the city center and then waited to get on the boat.

After a while, we began boarding. I proudly stepped onto the boat. We made our way to the top deck. The boat started moving. We were going down the river. I stepped outside from the indoor passenger deck to get some air. We were passing by the Hungarian Parliament Building. It's so beautiful. I've never seen the American White House, but I'm confident that the Hungarian Parliament Building is a million times prettier. This building was unbelievably big, like a palace. The Hungarian flag on its roof really stood out. The building was illuminated at night, which gave it a romantic feel. Then we passed under bridges, admired the castle, and saw the city in all its glory. I stood there, shocked by all this beauty.

We filmed an interview during our river tour. I was about to burst from all the emotions I was feeling. The boat turned around. I was enjoying every moment of it.

We docked. I thanked Tom and Delara for a beautiful evening. I was so tired that when we got back to the flat, I collapsed into bed and fell into a deep sleep.

Day 15

Exploring Budapest

During the night, some refugees from Odessa came to the apartment and stayed over. And earlier today, some other refugees arrived.

We're going to meet Delara and Tom later, and I'm going to read them my diary. I can't wait to see them. We decided to go for a walk, and both Granny and I felt a little more confident this time. We took a stroll around the green park. Today has been a warm and sunny day. The rest of the Channel 4 News crew is in Moldova already.

After our walk, we returned to the apartment and Tom and Delara came by to film me reading from my diary.

Every day, I text and call my friends. I ask them what the situation in Kharkiv is. I talk to my Granny Zyna and Granddad Yosip.

Tomorrow is a big day. I've been keeping a secret from this diary since soon after we met the reporters. Tomorrow, everything shall be revealed. . . .

IRELAND

"From Ukraine to Ireland: 12-year-old refugee Yeva reaches safety after Russia's invasion."

—Channel 4 News, Ireland, March 18, 2022

Day 16

I'm Flying Away

Today, I'm leaving for Dublin, Ireland. I've been keeping that fact from this diary so far! So let me explain. Since the very first day I met them, I've been asking the reporters to help us get to England. After about three days, it became clear that in order to do so, we'd need to have family there. They said we could go to Ireland or France instead. We'd heard that the people of France aren't very welcoming toward immigrants, and we don't speak any French. So we decided to go to Ireland.

During our phone conversation, Nik explained the process and sent us a document. The reporters were helping us along the way, and it was no accident that we ended up in Budapest. We got our plane tickets yesterday—Tom and Delara showed them to us on their phones.

We decided to go for a walk in the park and then go to a shopping center. We met up with Tom and Delara there. We sat down at a café and talked. At first, they said they'd come with us to Ireland, but now they were saying they can't after all. They walked us back to the apartment. We began packing. Then we sat down for the road before we set off for the airport.

We arrived and went inside. Everything was arranged for us and we were handed our tickets. Once we reached the security check, we said our farewells to the reporters, and they told us to reach out to them if we needed help with any-thing. We went through security and ended up in the depar-ture lounge. We sat around waiting for our gate number to be announced.

An hour went by. The gate number appeared on the screen—B24. We made our way to border control. Once through, we located our gate. All we had to do then was wait.

Our flight was delayed. We were supposed to depart at 8:20 p.m.

We stood in a line for half an hour. Finally, it started mov-ing. Staff checked our boarding passes and asked us to put our masks on. I searched through my pockets. No mask—no flight. There might be a war happening, but COVID hasn't gone anywhere. I was beginning to worry that this one tiny thing could mean us missing our plane. But thank God, it was all sorted out. The flight attendant gave us some masks. I was about to give in to despair. The line began slowly moving along onto the plane.

We spent a lot of time waiting for the airplane to take off. Finally, it started moving. I picked up my phone and began filming. The airplane picked up speed as it traveled down the runway. Finally, we took off! It was awesome! I felt so happy, because I was going to a safe country and because there were people waiting to meet us at the airport.

I phoned the people who are going to host us in Dublin, Catherine and her husband, Gary, before takeoff. They were waiting to meet us at the airport. The flight took 2 hours and 40 minutes. I couldn't wait for us to get there.

Finally, the plane landed. We had arrived in Dublin! I took my phone off flight mode and saw that it was bursting with messages. I wanted to reply to them all, but I wasn't connected to the Internet.

We left the airplane and walked through many long corridors. It felt like we were going in circles to get to border control. Once there, there was a problem with Granny's papers, but it all got worked out and she was given a visa allowing her to stay for ninety days. We'll sort out the rest later. For now, we were just trying to find our way out of the airport. Someone was expecting us. . . .

We asked for directions to the exit. We walked through the doors and . . . there was a crowd of people awaiting our arrival. There were television reporters, our hosts' friends and family, and our hosts themselves—Catherine and Gary. It was a warm welcome. We kept hugging each other. I'm very happy.

11:00 p.m. Now we're going to go find the car and head to the house. The Irish are very kind and friendly. By the way, they drive on the left side of the road here.

When we got into the car, I called the Channel 4 News crew and thanked them for all their help laying out this path for us, for the wonderful hosts they found, and for making us feel safe.

We arrived very late, at midnight. There's a dog at the house called Buddy. I gave him some cuddles. We were shown around the house and to our room. I was showered with gifts—a new set of pajamas, some makeup, some gym clothes, and some toys. I was so excited I couldn't get to sleep until 3 a.m.!

Day 17

Warm Welcomes

Today is a brand-new day in a brand-new country. I met our new neighbors and they welcomed me warmly to Ireland. We hugged. They were so happy to see us. Even though Granny doesn't speak any English, she could see how sincere these people were. Some brought flowers. Others brought gifts. It was such a lovely feeling.

We sat and talked. They were very interested in our story. Then one of the neighbors asked if I wanted to go over to her house to play their piano. I was glad to, but had not played anything in almost a month. At first, I struggled to remember how to play any of the music I had learned, but soon it all came flooding back to me. Hearing the sound of a piano again felt wonderful. It was such a joy to play some classical music.

7:00 p.m. In the evening, more neighbors came by, and they had a daughter my age. Her name was Nina. She asked if I wanted to go do some baking with her. I really love baking all sorts of tasty things, so I said yes!

We had fun talking as we mixed the ingredients. Together, we put the scones in the oven and then went to play a game of Kimble with her mom, which was a lot of fun. I was very pleased because I won.

Once we were done playing, it was time to take the scones out of the oven. They were pretty. And then I needed to get back to Catherine and Gary's house. What a fun evening! I brought some of the scones to share and everyone liked them. They were just so tasty!

Day 18

The Irish Sea

This morning, some Irish reporters filmed an interview with me, which was going to be on the TV that evening. This was the first time I saw myself on television. It didn't make me feel much, though. Inside, I'm just in pain.

After that, we went to a Ukrainian Catholic church to attend Mass. We prayed for ourselves and for everyone we love back in Kharkiv.

Gary came to fetch us, and I was pleased to see he had Buddy in the car with him. He asked if we wanted to go for a walk along the beach by the Irish Sea. We jumped at the chance!

When we arrived, I could feel the wind on my face and blowing through my hair. We climbed down to the beach and it was low tide, which made the beach look huge. I took some pictures. The sea was breathtakingly beautiful. I was all wrapped up in a snug, warm coat, but kite-surfers were there, rushing bravely into the water, not minding the cold one bit! They were fascinating to watch, gliding over the waves. The sea was like a mirror reflecting the sky. I ran around on the sandy beach, enjoying every wonderful moment. I felt over-whelmed with emotion. Buddy was zooming around too, and I kept trying to catch him. It was so thrilling.

Then we went to take a look around the city. Trees are planted along the bank. Gorgeous green parks that you can actually run around on!

When we got home, the puppy was completely spent. It was a truly beautiful day.

Day 20

News from Kharkiv

Yesterday, we phoned my other grandparents. They told us they've moved basements and are currently holed up underground somewhere on Haharina Avenue in the south of Kharkiv. It was a far more comfortable setup, with spaces to sleep, wash up, cook, and eat. I felt relieved for them, because their last basement was a very unpleasant, damp place.

Marfa, Granny's friend, went to fetch some bread and met some people giving out humanitarian aid, but the next day, when she left the basement again, she saw that everything had gone; it had been destroyed in the bombing.

8:00 a.m. Today I visited Gary's school, where he teaches. I met the other girls there; they were older than me, but we still had fun together.

The entire group then left the school and got on a train. I could see Dublin through the window. The curious thing about Dublin is that there aren't any buildings taller than five stories here. European-style streets. Stunning redbrick buildings. It surprised me that the city doesn't have a metro!

We walked over a bridge that straddles the River Liffey—it's amazing. I'm looking around and seeing many different bridges. Some are tall, large, and built to allow cars to drive over them. But others are small, for pedestrians only. We walked along

Dublin's best-known street—Grafton Street—and then we walked along the river and made a turn toward EPIC, the Irish Emigration Museum. We kept together, like a row of geese.

Then we entered the glass building of the EPIC Museum. We got our "museum passports," fun little booklets with a map of the museum's exhibits, which you can mark off with a stamp as you visit them. We went inside. There was a lot of information about the history of Ireland to take in, and I couldn't always understand everything. We learned about the history of the courts, the famine, the wars, national holidays, Irish food and dance. I tried doing some of the moves. I don't mean to brag, but I think I was actually quite good at it!

After the museum, we made our way to Trinity College. On the way, I was amazed by how pretty all the streets and shops looked. And then we stepped inside the library and saw the ancient Book of Kells. It's very big, 1,200 years old, and written in Latin. We weren't allowed to take photos. Then we walked up some stairs and entered a very long library. Two stories filled with books. I had no doubt you could find a few of Pushkin's poems there (that's whose name popped into my head when I tried to think of a writer, I don't know why). Someone played the theme music from Harry Potter on their phone, and right away I imagined I was at Hogwarts.

On our way back to the train, I saw a beautiful bus, sort of like the ones they have in London, but more colorful. When I finally arrived back at the house, I was so tired I could barely put one foot in front of the other. I crashed out with Buddy cuddled up on top of me. Happy, I fell into a deep sleep.

Day 21

Svyatohirs'k Destroyed

I'm enjoying being here, but today I was overcome by sadness. I miss home, I miss my friends, I miss my school.

Catherine took me to the school where she teaches. My sadness gradually disappeared, and I had another try at Irish dancing with the girls there. The school lessons were fun. During playtime, we went out onto the green courtyard. I need to improve my English. I tried reading a book in English at the library, but I had quite a bit of trouble and couldn't understand much, so I had to use the translator app. I'm not too worried, though—I'll learn.

I had a wonderful day in Dublin, but it was a horrible day in Kharkiv and in the Donetsk Oblast.

There used to be a huge shopping center next to my school, but not anymore. Today it was destroyed. There's a rumor that they're going to start using chemical weapons against remaining survivors. That's basically genocide against the Ukrainian people at this point!

There's a famous city in Ukraine called Svyatohirs'k. It has a beautiful monastery. I visited there just last summer, relaxing and enjoying life, and today it was bombed. Destroyed.

Day 22

My First St. Patrick's Day

Today, our friends the Channel 4 reporters are going to come to Dublin because it's St. Patrick's Day. I was delighted! We're going to go see the parade, and we have to wear something green.

Catherine and I are making cupcakes with green frosting. I tried the frosting mix and . . . my teeth turned green! I spent five minutes trying to decide whether or not to brush them again. I was still making a decision when I heard the doorbell. That was very awkward.

But I quickly brushed my teeth and they were white again. Phew!

I came out into the hallway and saw that Paraic and the crew were there. We hugged. I'd missed them.

When we got to the parade, the reporters began filming. I made my way through a small crowd to get a better look. There were so many different people. Soldiers, musicians, acrobats—anyone you could think of. There were also people dressed as characters from Irish history and folklore, but we didn't know who any of them were—yet. I watched with delight, so excited to see who would come around the corner next.

The parade was almost over and we were getting ready to leave, but Paraic was nowhere to be seen. We set off together

Here I am at my first St. Patrick's Day parade, in Dublin, March 17, 2022.

to search for him. Just as I was beginning to feel that we'd searched through half the city center, Paraic finally turned up.

Then we saw a couple wrapped up in Ukrainian flags. We talked to them. Turns out they'd only arrived in Dublin a couple of days ago.

One of the biggest questions I had for them was "Were there lots of airplanes in the sky where you were? How did you cope with the terrible noise?"

They said, "On the very first day, as we ran, we saw airplanes fly over our heads. After that we moved countries five times before deciding to come to Dublin." It wasn't a long conversation, but everything came back to me: the good and the bad. I felt sadness and pain. Tears welled up in my eyes. I remembered how I cried as I prayed for my home to be spared from the bombs. I thought of Kharkiv and all the important things in it that have now been destroyed.

When I got into the taxi to go home, tears started rolling down my face.

Day 25

Each Day Weighs Heavier on My Soul

I want to dedicate today's diary entry to my friends and family who are still back home. Our friend Marfa has told us that it is painful to talk about what has become of Kharkiv.

She says an apartment building next to the hospital clinic was on fire. The district heating offices have been wiped off the face of the earth.

Granny's friend Anzhela sent us a video of the kindergarten near our apartment—it's been bombed. We hope the apartment itself is all right.

My neighbor fled to Germany with her mother. Granny's friend Nelya fled to Poland, together with her son. My grandparents are still holed up in the basement on Haharina Avenue in Kharkiv. My aunt and uncle are in Poltava, together with my cousin.

We called Motrona. She works at a funeral home and said she was in the middle of a funeral procession when shelling started up. She's afraid for her life.

Day 28

I Am Hurting for Kharkiv

The war has been going on for a month now. It has brought so much suffering to my friends and my family—to everyone. How many lives has this war taken already, and how many more is it yet to claim? No one knows what will happen tomorrow, or in an hour, or even in a minute. . . . But the fewer people who know what war is, the better we'll all be. The world would be a happier place, because there's nothing worse than war.

Every day, my heart gets torn to pieces as I watch what's happening in my home country, in my hometown. Those who survive the war will never be the same as before. They will enjoy life and enjoy their days again, but only because it's a day without war. Now they know, and will forever know, what it's like to wake up to the sounds of shelling and missiles. And what it's like to pray for their home every day. Today your home wasn't hit by a missile, but tomorrow things might be different.

Every day there are more and more residential blocks being bombed. And I'm growing more and more tired of asking *Why are you fighting? Who's going to rebuild all of this and how long will that take? Why did you need to start this?* We were living in peace and harmony!

What pains me most is how many innocent civilians and children are getting killed. The Russian army are ruthlessly launching their bombs, wiping cities off the face of the earth.

March 18

A Journey into Dublin

Today we went to the zoo. I was excited. I was very interested to see what the zoo in Dublin is like.

We got in the car and drove off into a large park. It had green open spaces and small thickets. I wanted to get out of the car and run around on the grass. The park was so vast that it would take an entire day to explore it all. The president of Ireland has a house somewhere in this park, but we never went to it.

The park was great, but that was just the tip of the iceberg. The zoo was incredible! The lemurs jumped around in the trees like they never even suspected they were living in a zoo. They were all different colors: there were red ones and gray ones and black ones too. The tiger was teasing everyone by hiding behind some trees, forcing everyone to wait around for it to come out. Meanwhile, the lions were lying out in the sun without a care in the world. The sea lions kept popping their heads out of the water before diving back down again. There were about seven giraffes huddled together, trying to nudge their way to some leaves. The gorillas were hanging out on their island, deep in conversation. We nearly got lost in a bamboo grove on our way to the elephant enclosure. I couldn't get over how huge the rhinoceros were.

We were about halfway through the route when it got really pretty. There was an artificial waterfall that glistened in the sun. There was a lake, surrounded by a small jungle with monkeys jumping from tree to tree. A small bridge took us over the lake and onto a little island. I wanted to climb over the railing and go play with the monkeys on their island, but I was becoming really tired, so I couldn't have even if it was allowed! It was getting harder to walk. I was enjoying the zoo, but I hadn't any energy left. We didn't have time to see everything, but the things we did see were incredible.

With each day, Dublin is getting more and more interesting. More and more amazing.

March 20

The Castle and the Field

Over the next few days, we became real tourists. We went to Malahide Castle, to different parks, beaches, and towns.

We went to a park. The blue sky was full of different shades, and the white clouds lay flat across the sky, just like they do in a painting. The green lawn was perfectly cut. It was so pretty that I instantly felt the urge to go run around on it. The whole place had a smell of freedom.

We parked the car and headed toward a tall pine forest. Then we made our way to the castle. I caught a glimpse of one of its towers in the distance. It looked like something from medieval times. We turned a corner, and Malahide Castle appeared before us in all its glory. It was built more than 830 years ago, but it still looks stunning. I turned around and saw a wide clearing behind us. I ran, holding onto Buddy's leash. The poor guy kept tripping over himself as he struggled to keep up. I lay down on the grass and put my arms around him. I felt free.

Gary thought we could go to Portmarnock Beach next, near where he grew up.

There, sky-blue waters and sandbars stretched out into the distance. There were people there taking a stroll, and it seemed to me like they were walking over the sky.

We climbed down some stairs. The tide was out. There were little rock pools reflecting the sunlight, making it look as if they were covered in ice.

The sun was going down, and the sky was incredibly beautiful. The waves slammed against the rocks. There was a breeze coming from the sea. I thought I'd have an adventure and climb the rocks. They were slippery. Just as I was getting confident, Granny yelled at me to get back down to take a photo. I was very disappointed because I'd gone through all that trouble to climb across, and it was all in vain. I took in the splendid horizon. The blue of the water, the sky painted pinkish-purple and bluish-white. It was magnificent. I couldn't stop looking at it, but it was time to go back.

All of that was wonderful and beautiful, but every night before bed we watch the news about Ukraine and Kharkiv. The shelling continues. The Grads and missiles make us feel desperate. My family is hiding in a shelter. It's horrible and frightening to think about.

March 28

The Email

The moment has come for our reporters to move on to other stories. The Channel 4 News crew sent me an email that said that we won't be hearing from them for the foreseeable future. There are times when they focus on stories about specific people, but there are also times when they must work on other important assignments. It's reassuring for them to know that we are in a safe country now. The fact that they must now focus on other things might be difficult for everyone to accept, because it might seem like they're moving on, leaving behind those they've met along the way. But that couldn't be further from the truth. They shall never forget us . . . and we shall never forget them. I hope that we shall remain friends forever. . . . I sent them a letter, in English:

> *Dear Paraic and all the team at Channel 4 News,*
>
> *You are the kindest people who we could have met in our lives. You changed our lives for the better, and I don't know what would have happened if we had not met you. You rescued us from the war and saved our lives. This was a great deed and not many people would have done this in the same*

situation. Any problems that we have now, I think, will be solved and everything will be great. Also, I want to say thank you for your help in finding a good literary agent. Maybe, I will meet her soon and my diary will find its own publisher (I never dreamt this would happen before I met you). I believe we will stay friends forever and ever (even if we don't keep in touch with each other often). I really hope we will meet again someday.

I send you lots of good wishes. Thank you seems like too small a word to say for everything you have done for us.

Yeva and Iryna

March 29

The Lighthouse

This trip has changed everything I thought I knew about traveling. For a few seconds today, I was transported to Sochi. It's where my great-grandmother lives—a seaside town in Russia. I saw some palm trees, and they seemed so odd here that I felt like there was a bit of Sochi here. I used to spend entire summers there, splashing around in the sea, but the war has divided Russia and Ukraine. It's so sad.

We followed a winding road all the way to the very top of Howth (a small mountain). We got out of the car, and a beautiful view of the sea opened up before us. We made our way down a path and saw a lighthouse at the very edge of the coast. It was surrounded by cliffs, relentlessly battered by the surf. The waves raced each other, triumphantly crashing against the rocks. And the lighthouse stood there, quietly watching over the ships. The ships went by, one after another. The weather was amazing, not a cloud in the sky. If you took a boat straight from here, you could reach Wales. We got to the edge and it seemed liked there was no end to the sea. A boundless horizon. I sat down on a warm little boulder and looked out. . . . But at the same time, I felt such sorrow. . . .

April 1

First Day at School

Today was my first day at an Irish school. I was excited. As soon as I woke up, I pulled on my new teal school uniform. We got in the car and drove all the way across Dublin to get to the school. There was a lot of traffic, but as we drove over the bridge, I felt excited to be a part of it all. Little cars going about their business—like bees in a hive. And the sun was calling for everyone to get out of bed. The city was coming alive.

School started at 8:30 a.m. Phew! I made it on time. My new classmates welcomed me and were all very friendly. I attended each class eagerly, my face glued to the translator app. Everything's in English. I had to switch from what I had been learning at my Ukrainian school to the Irish curriculum, and do it all in a different language too. It's an all-girls school, and I made many friends. It was all very exciting. New teachers. Green tennis courts. There are grand pianos here that I can play music on. A huge library. And the school grounds are beautifully kept. Awesome!

My new friends and teachers were nice, but I missed my old ones. The war has forced us all to scatter across the globe.

Me in my new Irish school uniform on the first day of school!

People are fleeing Kharkiv every day. Our friend Marfa is no exception. Since the start of the war, she and her family kept having to move from one basement to another. Like tin soldiers, they held on for as long as they could, not wanting to leave home. Every day, they hoped for all this to be over soon. But everything changed in an instant. A missile hit very near where they were staying, killing a child and scattering dead bodies all over the neighborhood. They knew they had to flee. Right now, they're looking for a team of volunteers to help get their large family (seven people) out of Kharkiv and into Dnipro.

I can't stand the word *refugee*. I never could. When Granny began referring to us as refugees, I immediately asked her to stop doing that. Inside, it made me feel ashamed. I've only just understood why. I'm embarrassed to admit that I don't have a home. . . . It's felt unbearable ever since we fled our apartment to go to the basement. My dream is that, someday soon, we'll have our own place again.

April 26

My Cat Chupapelya Is Safe

Things are finally easing a little bit, after almost two whole months of war! For two months now, our apartment has been standing there, bombed from two sides, with its windows shattered and doors blasted off. The worst part is that the shelling continued even throughout the Orthodox Easter celebrations. They have no shame! It is just too hard to bear!

When we finally realized that we should start getting what remained of our things out of the apartment, we asked around to try to find someone who could move our things from that dangerous place.

Eventually, Granny was given the number for a person called Trofym who could help us. He said he'd pick up anything we asked him to, even the chandelier, no problem. He had already moved out entire shops, cars, and apartments. All we had to do was tell him where to go to pick the stuff up from and where to drop it off, and he would go there first thing (provided there wasn't too much shelling) and grab everything he could.

Unfortunately, as I fled, I forgot to grab my oil paints (a New Year's present from Granddad), my favorite clothes, and, most importantly, my beautiful pink toy cat, Chupapelya!

Granny made a list of all the things she wants to be rescued from the flat and where to find them. She included my oil paints but she said that Chupapelya would be just fine. I was sad, but I hoped that he would rescue her anyway and take her to Granny's friend's place, along with the rest of our things. We agreed that early tomorrow morning, he would go and pick up our things.

But in the meantime, today he went to find our friend's car, to make sure that it's still in one piece and hadn't been stolen. He also dropped by both our and our friend's apartments to see what state they're in.

First he checked on our friend's car, and it was still where she left it. Its windows were shattered (from a blast wave), and the doors and trunk were slightly damaged. The front of the car, along with the hood, was fine, which meant that it was fit to drive, had it not been for the fact that the battery turned out to be stolen.

After that he went to our flat, and it was painful to look at, even though we were only looking at a photo on a phone screen. Trofym opened—unsealed even—the front door. Inside, the hallway, as I've mentioned before, was buried under heaps of debris and, lying on the floor, our expensive German refrigerator, and the wall was caved in. The wardrobe by the front door was blown to bits. Clothes everywhere. The bedroom windows were shattered, and the flowerpots were thrown off the windowsill. Lying on the bed was my toy cat Chupapelya. By some miracle, she had been spared.

The television in the living room was damaged. The sofa facing the hallway was also hit (quite badly). But our armchair, which stood right next to the hallway, was untouched. The living room was covered in a thick layer of dust.

6:30 a.m., Ukrainian time, is when Trofym will come by our apartment. I set Granny's alarm for 4:30 a.m. and we both went to bed.

∽

I was getting ready for school when Granny shared some good news: Trofym moved all of our surviving things. He even managed to get the six-foot-long chandelier from the hallway by cutting it from the ceiling, and he brought everything over to our friend Motrona. Most importantly, he also brought my oil paints and Chupapelya. Now she is safe with Motrona!

My joy knew no bounds. We will never be able to repay that man—words can't describe how grateful we are! Such a weight off my shoulders. . . .

May 1

A New House

We've been offered a house to rent! It's a small place near my new school in South County Dublin. It might not belong to us, but we don't mind that.

We went to have a look at it. It turned out to be a cozy little house with a garden. We were met by two kind women, Linda and Juliette. They showed us around. There are flowers everywhere. The best part is that it's only a five-minute walk from my new school.

I have a dacha in Vovchanks, outside Kharkiv—it's a big, beautiful house. There are a lot of orchard trees there, and loads of flowers too. There's a river nearby—Siverskyi Donets. I loved taking my shoes off and going down for a swim among the blooming white water lilies. In the evening, Granny and I would sit by the big fireplace and drink tea. In the autumn, I'd go for a walk in the tall pine and oak forest and forage for mushrooms. There were loads of different kinds! Butter mushrooms, penny buns, bay boletes, and chanterelles.

That's all great, but the Russian occupiers are there now. It's so sad.

We are grateful to the kind Irish people who have helped us find a new house.

Afterword

This concludes this part of my diary. I don't know how many more days, months, or even years this war is going to last. How many lives it will claim, how much heartbreak it will cause, how big a toll it will take and has already, remains to be seen.

To this day, there are people suffering in Kharkiv, and I am amazed that they have the strength and will to carry on. Since this war began, I have learned to truly value my life. Sooner or later, everyone gets to learn that lesson.

I've dreamt about the first day of the war many times. In the dream, I am about to leave to go somewhere safe, and with tears streaming down my face, I tell my classmates that we shall never see each other again.

In one terrible instant, life has turned upside down and taken a totally different direction.

Before the war, life had its problems, but it was still good. I remember rushing to get to school with my classmates. I remember trying to look pretty for the older boys. It was all as it should be. One day, I'm worn out from bowling at my birthday party. Suddenly, I'm worn out from having to dive down into the basement shelter time and time again, exhausted from the fear that every day of this war brings.

Perhaps, in many years' time, I shall see my classmates and relatives again. But for now, I am turning the page, and I'm making new friends and meeting new classmates. The most important thing I want to say is that I believe only a strong faith in God can bring miracles.

MY FRIENDS' STORIES

When the war began, my friends and I were all forced onto separate paths. Each of us experienced different situations and moments where we could have really used each other's support. Some of us fled the city on the very first day, some held on until the very last second, and others are still in Kharkiv even now. These are their stories.

Khrystyna's Story

February 24, 2022, 4:50 a.m. I shall remember the date and time forever. The terrified look in my mother's eyes and the confused tone of her voice as she kept saying, "Wake up children, get dressed, quickly now, come on . . . ."

I didn't hear the first explosion, but I heard the ones that followed and felt them with my entire being.

At 8 a.m., instead of cheerfully walking to school to meet my friends and learn new things, we were rushing to the basement of my mom's work. (Mom works as a nursery school teacher.)

We spent the next thirteen days living in that basement.

During the first three days, there were seventy people living there with us: adults, children, and old people. There were some vulnerable people who couldn't stand up on their own. There were also three dogs, and a cat named Businka. Every time there was heavy shelling or loud explosions, the animals would hide under a pile of blankets.

During those first three days, we would wake up early and leave the nursery to go home to wash and cook some food. We also just really wanted to be home. I spent every second missing it.

But then we stopped being able to return home. It was too dangerous to leave the basement. The lights went out, it got really cold, and there were fewer of us there, as those who were able to leave had left.

The first time it got really scary was when a missile hit a nearby apartment building and the windows got blown out by the blast. Before then, the explosions were somewhere far away. Now, every day, another flat would burn down, and every day, there were fewer and fewer of us in the basement. Many left because their homes had been destroyed. Others left simply because it was getting too cold in the basement and the young children were beginning to get sick.

In the morning, Mom, Dad, and Granddad would go to the shop to try to fetch what food they could find. We would sprinkle some sugar on a piece of bread and pretend we were having a slice of Kyiv cake with our tea.

We slept fully dressed on mattresses normally used by the nursery at nap time, but it was still very, very cold. Leaving the basement to get some fresh air was terrifying, especially if the shelling started while you were out there. You'd have to drop down to the ground. The shrapnel left marks on the school walls.

On day thirteen, the nursery was hit by a missile.

At that time, there were nineteen of us left in the basement—twelve adults, five children, and two very old men aged 89 and 93 who were not able to walk. Most people were too scared to come here because the area was under constant shelling, but Dad found some volunteers who agreed to help us get out. We drove off toward the city center, but it started getting bombed there too, and eventually, forty-three days after the war had begun, me, Mom, and my brother fled to Western Ukraine.

Some of my favorite people—Dad, Granny, and Granddad—stayed behind in Kharkiv. I miss them terribly and I love them very much.

My greatest wish is for there to be peace!

✍

When I read her story, I began to understand the value of a buttered slice of bread with sugar sprinkled on top, even if it's not actually a slice of Kyiv cake. I know how horrible it is to have to sleep in a cold basement. But honestly, when she described seeing homes being burned to the ground every day—that was pure hell. Wanting to go out for some air, if only for a minute, and suddenly getting caught in the shelling. Being forced to sleep in a cold, dusty basement. But the worst part is that Khrystyna spent over a month trapped in Kharkiv. I'm so sorry that her family is still in there and that only her mother and brother were able to flee to Western Ukraine with her. We have faith that we shall meet again one day.

Olha's Story

It had been an ordinary day. I was back home from school, doing my homework, chatting with my friends, playing with my cat. Toward the evening, I started to develop an earache. Mom and I decided that if the pain wasn't gone by morning, I wouldn't have to go to school. But my ear had nothing to do with why I didn't go to school the next day.

At 5 a.m., I was woken up by a terrible explosion, which I mistook for an earthquake at first. I was terrified and saw the look of horror on my parents' faces. I asked them about the explosions and they said war had begun. . . . I was in complete shock. My cat Busya was sat next to me, as if offering comfort, even though the explosions must have scared her too. We started filling up bags and water bottles. In a panic, I began scooping everything off the table into a bag, but I knew that there was no way we could take all of it.

The explosions were getting louder, and we were very frightened by the time we got down to the ground floor of our building. Down there, the explosions didn't seem so loud and it felt safer. Playing games on my phone made me feel like I was hiding behind a shield. I tried not to listen to the explosions, but they were deafening. However, despite the fear we felt, we kept trying to cheer each other up.

The phone calls and texts I was getting from my friends and family were also a good distraction. We stayed in the ground floor lobby of our building, but when things quieted down, we would go back home to grab a bite to eat or to fetch something we needed. The next day we went to the store, and we had to stand in line for three hours. We filled an entire basket with food, but they started shelling again. The lights cut out and we all ran down to the shop's shelter. Once it got quiet again, we rushed back home. That shop hasn't opened since.

With each passing day, it was getting more and more terrifying. We weren't running back up to our apartment as often because it was too frightening. We spent six days under constant shelling and explosions. It got especially terrifying when we heard airplanes flying in the sky and making turns right above us. That really frightened us. We couldn't bear to spend another night in the ground floor lobby, so we had to sleep down in the hallway. In the morning, we gathered our things, including my beloved cat, and left the city.

The next day, our apartment building had a bomb dropped on it. We still dream of coming home one day.

None of us could ever believe that a war had begun, so we all came up with different ways to explain the sound of explosions. I thought that it was noise coming from someone baling scrap metal, and Olha thought it was an earthquake. When I would call her, I couldn't understand how she could stay in the lobby instead of going to the basement. But it's good that she had some support and that she tried to distract herself by keeping busy, because it would have been easy to go crazy otherwise. I still can't imagine what would have happened if Olha and her family had spent just one more day in that lobby instead of leaving the city when they did. The news of that bomb hitting her building would have come as a terrible shock. Her cat is a good friend to her, and I firmly believe that, one day, I shall meet her in person in a peaceful Ukraine.

Kostya's Story

February 24, 2022: I shall remember that day forever! That was my last day at home! That was the day the war started.

I was woken up by explosions. One, two . . . a third . . . My parents woke up and couldn't understand what was happening. Only after looking out the window and seeing both the sky and the buildings by the beltway on fire did we realize that the worst had happened: war!

My little sister Tania was crying, and Mom was trying to calm her down. I was very scared! We were engulfed by fear! Once we were dressed, my parents tried to decide what to do next. Where to go? I just wanted to get as far away from the explosions as possible!

We drove down to the center of Kharkiv. My aunt works at a school there. A big, beautiful old building designed way back when by Beketov himself.

There were loads of people gathered in the basement. Everyone was anxious and confused; no one knew what to do and what would happen next. The grown-ups turned the school gym into a sort of room for me and the other children. Mats were thrown on the floor for us to sit and sleep on, and even though the mothers washed the floor, it was still very dirty and very dusty.

Later that evening, we were joined by people from the neighboring buildings. But they weren't alone; they had their pets with them. Now we had with us dogs, cats, and even a hamster. Practically a whole zoo!

Some people slept on benches and chairs in the basement with the animals, while we slept in the school gym—we felt pretty safe there.

We could hear the explosions, some loud enough to pierce our hearts. We began to be able to tell if an explosion was close enough for us to need to brace or if it was somewhere far away. On Day 6, we heard the sounds of airplanes, and we got really scared. The horror around us was growing worse and worse. We felt like our situation was hopeless.

We would always be accompanied by one of the parents when we would leave our "kiddie bunker" to go to the bathroom or canteen.

The parents did their best to cheer us up: they'd come up with different games and activities. For example, I learned origami. However, despite the adults' best efforts, some of the children would still cry—scared by yet another *boom*. We would all try to help get them to settle down. We lived as if we were one big family, even though some of us had never met before the war. We became each other's support systems.

We spent eleven days in the school basement before driving out of the city, together with my parents, Granny, and my cat, Gilbert. I was shocked and upset seeing all the buildings that had been destroyed from our car window. You don't see that sitting in a basement! I was very surprised by the huge number of cars leaving the city. We spotted our friends in one of them, and we even had a few minutes to catch up. The moms cried!

Right now, I am in Central Ukraine, where it's more or less safe. But every day, the air raid alarms make us jump. Some say you can get used to anything. No! You can't get used to this!

I want to return home, to Kharkiv! To see my friends and play outside without having to hide from constant sirens and explosions! To go back to school, to see my teachers!

But most of all, I want to see genuine smiles on my parents' faces again.

My soul trembled as I read Kostya's description of that morning, because his morning, like mine, was full of panic. Full of anxiety. I was especially sad for his little sister, because her normal childhood was interrupted by the arrival of wartime. I remember thinking that the city center, around his school, was safe, but I thought wrong. I can only imagine the Spartan conditions they were living in. Dirt and dust are neither comfortable nor pleasant. But it's nice that he had something positive—animals. Hamsters, cats, and puppies are great, but the war was never too far away. After the arrival of airplanes and aviation, it became more difficult to move about the school freely, and I know the tension Kostya felt all too well. After he finally fled to Central Ukraine, I fully agree that it's no use trying to get used to the sound of air sirens. I truly hope that his dreams come true.

Alena's Story

On the morning of February 24, I was awakened by a loud noise that sounded like an explosion. I jumped out of bed and ran into my parents' bedroom and saw that they were up too. All I was told was, "It'll all be all right, sweetie!"

I watched as Mom threw things into suitcases while Dad rushed out of the apartment to go to the nearest gas station.

The phone rang. It was my brother, asking where we were going. We decided to go to my grandmother's house. Before we left the apartment, I managed to grab the teddy bear—our family mascot. Once outside, all I could hear and see were the screams and tears of the people standing on the street.

Then I looked at my family and immediately felt better.

As there were a lot of us, we had to use two cars. The streets were packed; it was impossible to drive. But Dad knew a shortcut. I felt scared that I'd never come back home or see my friends again.

Finally, we arrived at Granny's house! It felt like it took an eternity to get here, even though it was only a ten-minute drive. The men went to get the basement in order, and Mom, together with my aunt, drove to the shop to get food. It felt like things had settled down, but then I heard the phone ring and it was for my uncle, who worked as a border guard. He was going to war! My aunt was wailing, and my brother, who had just recently completed his military service, took my uncle aside and told him he'd be going with him. My uncle replied that he should stay and protect the family instead, and then began saying his goodbyes. I looked at my brother, who had tears streaming down his face. This strong, thick-skinned person was crying like a small child! I was crying too, but then my uncle came up to me, gave me a big hug, and promised he would come back. He closed the door behind him and the room felt very empty all of a sudden.

Later, we heard another series of explosions. Everyone was grabbing their things and rushing to the basement. At first, we just stayed quiet and listened to the missiles flying over our house.

I was hugging my teddy, praying silently, believing that God would help us. My brother and my dad would go back out again from time to time to check the news. My aunt kept trying to reach my uncle, but he wouldn't pick up. We spent the rest of the day sitting in the basement, until the explosions finally died down. Then we went back to the house to have something to eat and went to bed.

In the morning, I woke up thinking that it was all just a bad dream, but I snapped out of it as soon as I heard my brother yelling that there were explosions again. And that's the way it was, day after day. Up until the most horrifying day of my life.

The morning began as it usually would. We had breakfast and, at about 9 a.m., we heard the explosions again, so we rushed to the basement.

So here we were again, my whole family and my beloved teddy, hiding in the basement. I saw my father and brother go outside, and I hoped that meant we could go back to the house, where I could get back to reading my favorite Harry Potter book. But then I heard gunshots and a man's voice. They were ordering someone to surrender and said they only had one minute to do so. My brother and father ran back and told everyone to open their mouths and put their heads down. Immediately after, we heard explosions. That was the sound of my father's school, which he attended as a child, being blown up. The school survived World War II, but it didn't survive February 26, 2022.

After a while, the explosions had died down, and my brother and father left the basement, telling everyone to stay put. The was a strong smell of smoke in the air. When I was finally allowed to go outside, I thought I had arrived in hell: everything around us was painted red and covered in ash. That was the school burning. That's what the most horrifying day of my life was like.

Each day was no different from the last: always bad news and explosions. But I never lost heart, because I had my teddy with me.

One day, my dad and my brother decided that we were going to leave Kharkiv, but they couldn't decide where we should go. But then I heard the phone ring again—it was my uncle. He was safe and sound! After my dad and brother spoke to him, they said we should collect our things and that we were expected somewhere. It was late by now, 4 p.m., and the curfew was coming up, but my brother insisted we should get in the car and drive.

We left Granny's, but that wasn't the end of our problems. The explosions had blown the windshield off my brother's car, and rain and snow were pouring in as we drove. We were afraid we wouldn't make it!

I think my prayers helped us. We arrived at my uncle's friend's place in a village outside the city. There were more than 20 people packed into that tiny house. They invited us to have some borscht and *pirozhki*. The night went by quietly and, for the first time in many days, I had a full night's sleep.

Next morning, we traveled until we reached Dnipro. There, we were met by some friends of my dad's. They fed us and found us a place to live. Now we live next door to them.

I really want to go home, to see my friends and, most of all, I just want to hug my uncle! I am a child from Ukraine, my name is Alena, I am twelve years old, and all I want is to have peace and be back at home!

❧

It pains me to see all this chaos around us. The tears, the sorrow, the hurry, the fear. But there's nothing more painful than watching a loved one go to war. Without knowing if they'll ever return. Just waiting to hear even a single word from them. When Alena talks about the time she left the basement and felt like she was in hell, I can't even imagine how scared she was for her life.

When a building (the school) survives five whole years during World War II but doesn't even last a week of war between two countries, how can that be? How? It was shocking to think how she and her family managed to drive without a windshield, with water pouring in. To me, her entire journey seemed horrible and unbearable. Everything that happened in Alena's basement, everything she heard while hiding in there, terrified, not knowing what was going on outside. But she had someone to support her—her teddy.

I just want to say this: we are all only children, and we deserve to live a life of peace and happiness!

Acknowledgments

February 24. That day changed my whole life. On that day, I began writing this diary. Sometimes when I would feel pain and fear, I would sit down and write in it. On these pages, I would share my feelings and it would help me cope. My goal was to put my experiences into writing so that ten or twenty years from now I could read this and remember how my childhood was destroyed by war.

I have met lots of different people since the beginning of the war. I'm grateful to many of them, but some of them I'd rather forget. Those terrible days had taken off a great number of masks.

Yeva and her Granny Iryna on Iryna's sixtieth birthday.

I want to dedicate these last pages of my diary to the kind people I've met as I lived through the difficult days of war.

My beloved Granny Iryna has always stood beside me. She supported and protected me since the very first minutes of the war. Even when my hands would shake with fear, I knew for certain that as long as I am with Granny, she will do everything in her power to keep me safe. I haven't been alive for all that long, but I've always trusted her. I'm so thankful for her.

On February 25, it was clear that we weren't safe in our home neighborhood and that we must flee. Granny reached out to all her friends asking for help, but everyone turned us away. Except Inna. She agreed to take us in and let us stay with her at her house where it was safe. I'm very grateful to her for taking care of me. She kept coming up with ways to distract me (drawing, cooking).

We couldn't find a way to flee Kharkiv, and it would seem that all hope was lost, but God sent us Todor and Oleh, two amazing volunteers who fearlessly agreed to take us to Dnipro. I thank them for their bravery and the kindness in their hearts. I met a lot of incredible people—Rada, Arsenyi, Myna, Father Emilio, Attila, Vera, and Motrona—these are all people with big, generous hearts.

The reporters from Channel 4 News—Paraic, Flavian, Tom, Delara, and Nik—have completely changed my life. When they heard my story and learned of this diary, they decided to help us in any way they could. They worked hard and, thanks to them, I was able to make it all the way to Dublin. Those amazing, kind, brilliant, and generous people are always prepared to help those in need. They have left a bright and warm little light deep within my soul.

In Dublin, we were welcomed by Catherine Flanagan and her family. After a long and difficult journey, my life had turned into a fairy tale. A beautiful house and a warm, cozy atmosphere. Gary, Catherine's husband, has shown us around all the beautiful parts of Dublin. Catherine helped me enroll at the school she works in. They helped us during a very difficult time in our lives, and I am thankful to them.

I was very well received at my new school. Here, I feel safe and at ease. As if I was always a student here. I'm free to play the grand piano or go to one of the tennis courts and play tennis. The girls in my class gave me a very warm welcome. I've made lots of new friends. I'm grateful for their kindness and sincerity.

I would also like to express my gratitude to the owners of the house we're now living in. It's a beautiful home in a beautiful place, and we're very happy here.

I'm so thankful to God for meeting an amazing, beautiful woman—Marianne Gunn-O'Connor. I could fill an entire chapter of this diary with how wonderful she is, but I'm especially grateful for her warmth, kindness, compassion, and desire to help. The world needs more people like her. Marianne has kindly offered to be my literary agent, which is a great honor.

I am especially grateful to Union Square & Co. for offering to publish this diary. Emily Meehan, Claire Wachtel, and Barbara Berger were the first to believe in me. This diary would not be possible without their support. With their help, I'm confident that things will work out for me. I'm so happy to be published by them.

I'm thankful to God and to the kind people I've met along the way. Everything will be all right. I believe that!